19.95

The TQM Paradigm

The Management Master Series

William F. Christopher
Editor-in-Chief

8

The TQM Paradigm

Key Ideas That Make It Work

Derm Barrett

PRODUCTIVITY PRESS

Portland, Oregon

Volume 8 of the *Management Master Series*
William F. Christopher, Editor-in-Chief
Copyright © 1995 by Productivity Press, Inc.

All rights reserved. No part of this book may be reproduced or utilized in any form or by any means, electronic or mechanical, including photocopying, recording, or by any information storage and retrieval system, without permission in writing from the publisher. Additional copies of this book are available from the publisher. Address all inquiries to:

Productivity Press
P.O. Box 13390
Portland, OR 97213-0390
United States of America
Telephone: 503-235-0600
Telefax: 503-235-0909

ISBN: 1-56327-073-0

Book and cover design by William Stanton
Cover illustration by Paul Zwolak
Typeset by Laser Words, Madras, India
Printed and bound by BookCrafters in the United States of America

Library of Congress Cataloging-in-Publication Data

Barrett, Derm.
  The TQM paradigm: key ideas that make it work / Derm Barrett.
    p. cm. – (Management master series; v. 8)
  1. Total quality management. I. Title. II. Series: Management master series; v. 8.
  HD62.15.B369 1995   94-42933
  658.5'62 – dc20   CIP

00 99 98 97 96 95   10 9 8 7 6 5 4 3 2 1

—CONTENTS—

Publisher's Message   vii

Acknowledgements   x

1. **Introduction   1**
   The Power of Ideas   1
   The TQM Revolution   2
   What Is an Idea?   2
   The Ideas of TQM   3
   Conceptual Thinking   4

2. **The Idea of Total   6**
   Quality without Boundaries   6
   The Scope of the Baldrige Award   6

3. **The Idea of Quality   8**
   International Comparisons   8
   Quality versus Quantity   9
   Measuring Quality   10

4. **The Purpose of a Company   14**
   The Idea of Partnership   15
   Communication   16
   The Customer-Company-Supplier Chain   17

5. **Managerial Economics 19**
   Adding Value 19
   Process Improvement 20
   Activity-based Accounting 21
   Flowcharts 21
   Business Reengineering 22

6. **Time-based Management 24**
   The Customer's Time 24
   The Employee's Time 25
   Time Management Skills 25
   Cycle Time 26
   Time Flies 27

7. **The Systems Concept 28**
   The Socioeconomic System 28
   Systems, Connections, and Subsystems 29
   Thinking Holistically 29
   Living Systems 30
   Integration and Coordination 30
   The Human-Machine Interface 31
   The Stakeholder Idea 31

8. **Management 33**
   Discovery of the Management Process 33
   Strategic Management 35
   Juran Trilogy 37
   Plan-Do-Check-Act 37
   Scientific Management 38
   Technology Management 39
   Dionysian Management 41
   Quality Management 41

9. **Business Is People** 43
   Employees as Managers and Entrepreneurs 43
   Theory X and Theory Y 45
   Total Involvement 47
   Learning 47
   Teams and Teamwork 50
   Leaders and Leadership 50
   Three Dimensions 51

10. **Hyperchange** 53
    Outward Looking 54
    Change Responsive 55
    Focus on the Future 56

11. **Idea Generation** 57
    Creative Thinking Techniques 58
    Creative Thinking at Sony 62

12 **Summary** 63

Notes 64
Further Reading 65
About the Author 66

PUBLISHER'S MESSAGE

The *Management Master Series* was designed to discover and disseminate to you the world's best concepts, principles, and current practices in excellent management. We present this information in a concise and easy-to-use format to provide you with the tools and techniques you need to stay abreast of this rapidly accelerating world of ideas.

World-class competitiveness requires managers today to be thoroughly informed about how and what other internationally successful managers are doing. What works? What doesn't? and Why?

Management is often considered a "neglected art." It is not possible to know how to manage before you are made a manager. But once you become a manager you are expected to know how to manage and to do it well, right from the start.

One result of this neglect in management training has been managers who rely on control rather than creativity. Certainly, managers in this century have shown a distinct neglect of workers as creative human beings. The idea that employees are an organization's most valuable asset is still very new. How managers can inspire and direct the creativity and intelligence of everyone involved in the work of an organization has only begun to emerge.

Perhaps if we consider management as a "science" the task of learning how to manage well will be easier. A scientist begins with an hypothesis and then runs experiments to observe whether the hypothesis is correct. Scientists depend on detailed notes about the experiment—the timing, the ingredients, the amounts — and carefully record all results as they test new hypotheses. Certain things come to be known by this method; for instance, that water always consists of one part oxygen and two parts hydrogen.

We as managers must learn from our experience and from the experience of others. The scientific approach provides a model for learning. Science begins with vision and desired outcomes, and achieves its purpose through observation, experiment, and analysis of precisely recorded results. And then what is newly discovered is shared so that each person's research will build on the work of others.

Our organizations, however, rarely provide the time for learning or experimentation. As a manager, you need information from those who have already experimented and learned and recorded their results. You need it in brief, clear, and detailed form so that you can apply it immediately.

It is our purpose to help you confront the difficult task of managing in these turbulent times. As the shape of leadership changes, The *Management Master Series* will continue to bring you the best learning available to support your own increasing artistry in the evolving science of management.

We at Productivity Press are grateful to William F. Christopher and our staff of editors who have searched out those masters with the knowledge, experience, and ability to write concisely and completely on excellence in management practice. We wish also to thank the individual volume authors; Diane Asay, project manager; Julie Zinkus, manuscript editor; Karen Jones, managing editor; Bill Stanton, design and production management; Susan Swanson, production coordination; Laser Words, text and graphics composition.

Norman Bodek
Publisher

ACKNOWLEDGMENTS

I have a large debt of gratitude to four groups of people who made this book possible. The first group is the great thinkers who, through the power of their ideas, have made modern management evolve into what it is today, a complex system of concepts, ideas, and methods whose power is enormous when properly applied, as they are, for example, in advanced forms of TQM. A second group consists of the many mentors who have helped me to develop my own thinking and skills over a period of forty years of working with them. A third group consists of the many clients and students whom I have served and from whom I learned much more than they realize. A fourth group contains those friends and colleagues who have helped me work on the book itself.

Most managers are well aware of the great economic thinkers, past and present, who have influenced the policies of modern states and governments, people like Malthus, Smith, Marx, Shumpeter, Marshall, Keynes, Friedman, Samuelson, Galbraith, just to list some familiar names. Their ideas have had an enormous impact on us all, sometimes without us appreciating just how great these impacts have been. Great thinkers in management have had a similarly powerful effect on the structure and functioning of our public and private institutions and organizations. The list includes names like Taylor, Gilbreth, Fayol, Follet, Simon, McGregor, Herzberg, Barnard, and

Drucker, among many others. These thinkers have had a profound effect on my perceptions and understandings of management and TQM, and I have described the ideas of quite a few of them in the course of this book.

The mentors whose influence on my thinking has been similarly profound are numerous. They count in the dozens. I would like to mention, though, four of my teachers in the Department of Economics and Social Science at MIT: Doug McGregor, Alex Bavelas, Joe Scanlon, and Rupert McLaurin.

Doug made me aware of the immense desire that the average worker has to do a quality job, take on responsibility, and exercise creative thinking and ingenuity, if only management will allow her or him to do so. Alex helped me see into the dynamics and interactions of people who work in teams and small groups and gain an appreciation of the power of teamwork and collaboration. Joe helped me discover how employees can successfully cooperate with management, at an equal level, to produce remarkably great gains in productivity, profit, and quality. Rupert revealed to me the great drama of economic growth and progress; he taught me that economies move forward principally as a result of the heroic contributions of entrepreneurs, inventors, innovators, and managers working in orchestrated effort.

In addition, the lectures and books of Norbert Weiner, the MIT mathematician who invented cybernetics, guided a lot of my own research and teaching while I was at MIT. Norbert Weiner gave me a view of how complex goal-oriented systems such as companies and other organizations operate by processes of goal-setting, communication, feedback, and control. I had the good fortune to be exposed to these great thinkers and teachers during the late 'forties and early 'fifties while I was still in my twenties. I find it gratifying that the ideas of these original thinkers of the forties are now gaining the wide currency they deserve, and are being widely applied. They are all among the greats in the history of organizational and managerial thought.

My forty years of teaching and consulting have been a great adventure and an enormous source of learning and pleasure. I've loved both consulting and teaching passionately. I've had the very good luck to teach at a number of different universities in Canada and the United States and to have consulted with dozens of organizations in both the private and public sectors. The consulting has taken me to different continents and countries and into every form of organization from armies to hospitals and aluminum companies to retail stores. Consulting is a form of "action learning." Every case is different, and either confirms old knowledge or produces surprises and new insights. My clients have included many dedicated, talented, and intelligent persons from whom it is impossible not to learn a lot. I hope some of their wisdom has found its way into the pages of this book.

The friends and colleagues who helped me directly with the manuscript for this book include first of all Tina Barrett, my partner in our consulting firm of Management Concepts Limited. Tina and I are marriage as well as business partners, and she has worked actively with me at all stages of the book. She played a critical role in helping to design the structure and thrust of the book. Tina also reviewed every paragraph and chapter and made suggestions for improving their content and clarity. To a considerable extent, it is her book as well as mine. My colleagues John Wilson and Stephen Leahey are also to be emphatically thanked for their suggestions on the draft manuscript. Bill Christopher, the editor of the *Management Master Series*, asked me to write it in the first place and then provided me with comments and suggestions as it proceeded. Finally I want to thank Norman Bodek, Diane Asay, and others at Productivity Press for making it possible for me to write the book and have it edited, printed, and put in the hands of the reader.

Derm Barrett
Scarborough, Ontario
August, 1994

1
INTRODUCTION

To understand TQM is to understand the ideas behind it—the great ideas on which it rests and that give it power. This book provides a bedrock understanding of TQM ideas in a brief, clear format. Total Quality Management works well when everyone understands the ideas. Yet many companies embark on a TQM strategy without that understanding. To be sure, implementing TQM requires more than ideas. The organization has to commit to making it work. They must take action and use TQM techniques. Everyone has to receive training. In the final analysis, however, the vital force is the ideas themselves. Understand the ideas and you can make TQM work.

THE POWER OF IDEAS

The modern world owes its character and content to the great ideas that created it. Some are early engineering ideas like the pulley and the lever. Some are later ideas like the train and the airplane, or more recent ones like space travel and electronic networking. Some are early business ideas like agriculture and trade or later ones like mass production and interchangeable parts. Some are recent like strategic alliances and horizontal organization. Some are early biomedical ideas like plaster casts. Some are later ones like hygiene or very recent ones like gene splicing. Some are early political ideas like law and order or later ones like democracy and freedom. Some are recent like universal human rights and multiculturalism. These are historically great ideas that created change and made things happen. They were driving concepts. They made the world a different place.

THE TQM REVOLUTION

Today, the application of the great ideas contained in TQM is writing a new chapter in business history. TQM is creating a revolution in manufacturing, in mining, and in transportation; in telecommunications and in banking; in hospitals, hotels, and the food industry; in schools and in federal governments; in state and provincial governments; in cities and municipalities; and in fire departments and police forces. Its sweep is extraordinary.

Wherever we apply the ideas of TQM, the effect is transformative. The TQM process creates new organizations with new qualities and new characteristics. This is not rhetoric, but reality. All we need to do is examine companies and institutions that have experienced the TQM renewal process. The evidence for a transformative revolution is there. It is visible in Motorola, G.E., Xerox, Ford, Saturn, and Federal Express, among many others.

WHAT IS AN IDEA?

An idea is not a physical force. It is a mental force — a construct of mind. Can something so intangible as an idea have the power to change the concrete facts of business? To answer that question, here are some examples:

- the assembly line in the auto industry
- mutual funds in the investment industry
- self-serve in retail

Great ideas have the power to change, improve, and transform business reality. But they demonstrate their power only when the people who use them also understand them. Ideas help us think, plan, and act intelligently and effectively. Because of ideas we can do things:

- The idea of a *circle* and the idea of a *square* allow us to choose which of these two shapes to use when we build a table.

- The idea of *teams* allows us to set up a team, say, a project team.

- The idea of *flexible hours* allows us to hire employees who otherwise would not be available.

- The idea of *feedback* (borrowed from electrical engineering) allows us to ask our customers for their thoughts on how to improve the quality of a product or a service.

The collective force of the great ideas contained in *Total Quality Management* allows us to do a huge number of things we could never do before. We can achieve a level of business excellence not otherwise achievable.

THE IDEAS OF TQM

The key ideas of TQM are not new, despite the impression sometimes conveyed. But, every one of them is a great idea that has stood the test of time. What is new is that applying all the ideas in concert dramatically affects the quality and level of business performance. TQM is the application in unison of the very best ideas in business. TQM ideas tie business facts into a pattern in which they become highly manageable. How they are able to do this becomes evident in this book.

TQM consists of three main ideas: total, quality, and management. These three main ideas lead to other TQM ideas like purpose, expectations, and customer satisfaction; continuous improvement and partnership; flowcharting, reengineering, and systems theory; future-focusing, hoshin management, and hyperchange; total involvement, teamwork, empowerment, and horizontal organization; goals and results, creativity and innovation, and many others. These are some of the ideas that this book addresses.

CONCEPTUAL THINKING

The ability to think in terms of ideas and their application is called conceptual thinking. The skill with which we think conceptually has become an increasingly important competitive resource as old facts become obsolete, change, and disappear. Daily, new facts supersede existing facts. These in their turn also disappear and are replaced. Nothing stays put, everything changes, moves, and shifts. Reality never stays the same, it flows on like a river in a torrent of ever-changing events. How do we understand what's happening when change becomes so rapid, radical, and revolutionary as it has become today? The answer is to draw on ideas and concepts that have explanatory ability.

Ideas and concepts help us see the patterns of order that surface ambiguities, anomalies, and contradictions hide. Conceptual thinking enables us to make sense of what is happening and arrive at the right decisions about what to do. If we don't exercise and apply our ability to think conceptually, we resort to using the same old approaches that are already failing. Or else we resort to quick-fix, one-minute formulas and popular flavor-of-the-month remedies. But, by really using our conceptual skills, we can get under the surface of things and work out intelligent solutions that actually produce results.

As the world becomes more complex, faster moving, and more turbulent, the need for conceptual thinking skills—the ability to use and create concepts and key ideas—becomes rapidly greater. More than ever before, today's organizations are on the lookout for executives with highly developed abilities for conceptual thinking. They recruit with that criterion in mind, and they train managers and employees who are already in place in concept formation and concept application.

2

THE IDEA OF TOTAL

The idea, *total*, requires a company to concern itself with the quality of everything: products, processes, programs, people, policies, productivity, service, ethics, creativity, innovation—everything. Decades ago, quality referred only to the quality of products. Then it came to include the quality of processes and services as well. It finally became clear that the pursuit of quality should apply to everything. *It should be total.*

QUALITY WITHOUT BOUNDARIES

In TQM quality is without boundaries. You cannot limit it and still be serious about it. So it's no surprise that TQM companies work hard to improve the quality of top-management leadership, corporate culture, stakeholder relationships, research, strategic thinking—everything. The name of the TQM game is *excellence across the board*. Restrict it to one or two areas like product quality or customer service and you destroy it. "Total" means *total*.

THE SCOPE OF THE BALDRIGE AWARD

Nothing more clearly reveals the breadth and scope of today's idea of quality than does the Baldrige Award. The Baldrige Award for quality, which Ronald Reagan established in 1987, bears the name of former U.S. Secretary of Commerce Malcolm Baldrige. There are three award categories: manufacturing, service, and small business. In order to earn the Baldrige award, companies are judged on seven wide-ranging standards of excellence:

- leadership
- information and analysis
- strategic quality planning
- human resources utilization
- quality assurance of products and services
- quality results
- customer satisfaction

3

THE IDEA OF QUALITY

Necessity is the mother of invention. Management's growing concern with quality and excellence stems from competitive necessity. It is necessary to compete and succeed in world-class competition. Jack Welch, the CEO of G.E., puts it this way, "If you can't meet a world standard of quality at the world's best price, you're not even in the game."[1] In a world of global trade, consumers in any country can pick and choose the products they buy from whatever source offers the best value—the best combination of quality and price.

INTERNATIONAL COMPARISONS

Quality surveys have become standard practice. International rating organizations such as Gallup do surveys that compare different countries and their quality performance. In 1994, one such survey put Japan first in manufactured goods, Germany second, the U.S. third, Britain fourth, France fifth, and Canada sixth.[2]

The necessity to compete, however, is not by itself a sufficiently powerful motivator. A company must also be permeated with a burning desire for *quality for its own sake*. How come? Simple. What we have to do, we often do reluctantly. What we want to do, we do with zeal. Quality has to become an internalized yearning, a value in its own right, a deeply felt desire.

QUALITY VERSUS QUANTITY

Historically, North America has been fascinated with its own vastness. It was a land of plenty, where lots of things were readily and easily available. And everything was big — big prairies, big lakes, big mountains, big skies, big trees. To redirect our values from a preoccupation with quantity, size, and amount to focus on quality and caliber has not been easy. Quantity asks "how many?" and "how big?" Quality asks "how good?" The move toward quality is a true paradigm shift. The desire for quality and the expectation of quality is a whole change in mind-set, an alteration in what people value. Consumers now have the idea of quality firmly fixed in their minds.

Not only is there an increasing desire for quality in place of quantity, but there is an aversion and fear toward some kinds of quantity: too many automobiles on the streets and freeways, too many people crowded together, too much asphalt, too much garbage, too many gadgets, too much food, too much fat, too much pressure, too much noise, too much anger.

As a result of the new desire for high quality — for excellence — most people nowadays, for example, care less for how big their car is than how good it is. They are likely to prefer owning two excellent TVs to three of average quality. They are not very impressed with the fact that their children go to school for more years (quantity) than they themselves did. They are more concerned about the quality of that schooling. The demand for quality originates more in public demand than in management initiatives. And it is this that drives the quality management movement in business and the public sector.

MEASURING QUALITY

Quality lends itself to grading, scaling, and ranking. The quality scale ranges from bad and poor at one end to mediocre in the middle and good or excellent at the other end. We use "excellence" to describe a company, product, or person (or anything else) that has an unusually high degree of primarily good qualities.

When the idea of quality first took hold, we mainly tried to improve the quality of products rather than the quality of services. For example, we tried to make automobiles safer, more reliable, more rustproof, and so on. Later, we began to be more concerned with the helpfulness, friendliness, and care that the sales person and the service operation offer.

How does a supplier of a good or service determine good quality or bad quality? In the past, the overwhelming tendency was for producers to answer that question themselves. TQM, with its idea of partnership with and respect for the customer, concentrates on finding out what the customer judges quality to be. It then proceeds to meet, and perhaps exceed, that particular expectation. The company may, for example, manufacture cars that meet the quality expectations associated with a Jaguar or those associated with a Volkswagen. In either case, the TQM company tries to provide the kind of qualities and the level of excellence each type of customer wants.

Subjective Factors

Quantity is an objective thing. For example, how many dollars a person earns is not a matter of opinion. Quality is more subjective. For example, preferring a modernistic house to a traditional design is a matter of subjective taste and preference.

On the whole, services have more subjective elements than do products. But objective elements are still important in establishing the quality of a service. Think of the mileage Pizza Pizza gets from its delivery guarantee—thirty minutes or your money back. Or think how satisfied McDonald's customers feel when (as a result of a technological breakthrough) they can get a freshly baked pizza only four minutes after it goes into the oven.

Even so, fast delivery may not always be the issue. Some customers feel that one or the other company makes better pizzas. It's a matter of subjective taste and preference. It's easier to measure the objective than the subjective aspects of quality. But often subjective elements are the most important to the customer. The workable combination is something every company has to sort out.

Every company risks paying more attention to objective factors because they are more visible and measurable. The price for neglect of subjective factors, however, can be devastating.

The RATER Concept

Researchers Len Berry, Parsu Parasuraman, and Valerie Zeithaml have discovered some interesting things about how customers evaluate the quality of a firm's service. Customers tend to compare service performance as they *perceive* it with what their *expectations* were, that is, what they thought it *ought to be*. A *service quality gap* is said to exist when service performance falls short of customer expectations.[3]

Through interviews with business executives and customer focus groups, these researchers have developed a set of five useful, customer-centered criteria for evaluating the quality of a service. The criteria are:

- Reliability
- Assurance

- Tangibles
- Empathy
- Responsiveness

The acronym is RATER.

As an example, the researchers apply the criteria to telephone companies. Customers expect that when excellent telephone companies promise to do something by a certain time, they will do it (reliability). The behavior of employees of excellent telephone companies instills confidence in customers (assurance). Excellent telephone companies have modern equipment (tangibles). Excellent telephone companies have the customer's best interests at heart (empathy). Employees of excellent telephone companies are never too busy to respond to customer requests (responsiveness).

We need to develop other kinds of quality criteria and measurements for other areas. Such areas include financial management, innovation, technology, leadership, ethics, public responsibility, and human relationships.

Benchmarking

One of the great ideas in TQM is benchmarking. Using benchmarking, you can get a better idea of what is possible by looking at what some of the best players in the world have been able to accomplish. When Roger Bannister broke the four-minute-mile record for running he created a new idea of what was possible. Before that nobody believed it could be done. Now nobody knows what the limit is.

Whatever your company does, chances are someone else has done it better. So find out what's really possible. Benchmarking takes place in two steps:

1. Find out what the best practices and processes are in business *anywhere in the world*.

2. Adapt, improve, and implement your findings in your own firm. The ratio of the benefits to the costs of benchmarking is high, usually greater than five to one. That's hard to beat!

Benchmarking usually requires creative imagination rather than simple copycatting. It can take some interesting twists. When Xerox visited L.L. Bean, Inc.'s warehouse in Freeport, Maine, it picked up several good ideas for improving its order-filling processes. But, when Chrysler visited the Bean warehouse, what impressed Chrysler was that some of Bean's best warehousing ideas came from Bean workers, not just its managers. As a result, Chrysler went away with the idea that it too should start relying more on employees' abilities to solve problems.[4]

4

THE PURPOSE OF A COMPANY

In order to understand anything, we need to know its purpose. The purpose of a car is transportation. The purpose of a hammer is to drive in nails. The purpose of the lungs is to supply the body with oxygen. What is the purpose of a company? TQM companies believe their purpose is to satisfy customer needs and wants. Only if they succeed in this fundamental purpose will they continue to survive, earn a profit, and keep people employed.

Consequently they get close to their customers, and stay close. They design and deliver products and services that are aimed at delighting the customer. They constantly improve the quality and the value of products and services and add to them. They constantly invent new, better, and different products and services for the customer. They constantly seek out new customers to serve.

All organizations have customers and clients whose needs they exist to serve. The hospital exists to serve the patients—not the board, not the doctors, not the nurses. The school exists to serve the students—not the teachers, principals, or janitors. The purpose of government is to serve the people—not the elected representatives or the bureaucrats. Often those in power make the organization serve their own purposes. When TQM is introduced into such organizations it returns the organization to its original purpose. Hospitals start making the care of the patient the primary objective. Schools start putting the student first. Federal, state, provincial, and local bureaucrats start to serve the people rather than exploit or bully them.

THE IDEA OF PARTNERSHIP

A company alone is not a business. The TQM organization regards the customer as *a part of* the business, not as someone *apart from* the business. And there is no business until the company connects with customers and stays connected. Only then can business transactions take place.

What Is a Business?

A business is a union, a partnership, of two central parts: The company and the customer. (See Figure 1.) TQM companies base their entire existence on this two-part view of the nature of a business enterprise.

The Customer's Role in Business

How does the customer side of the partnership work? The customers supply all the revenue. Without revenue the

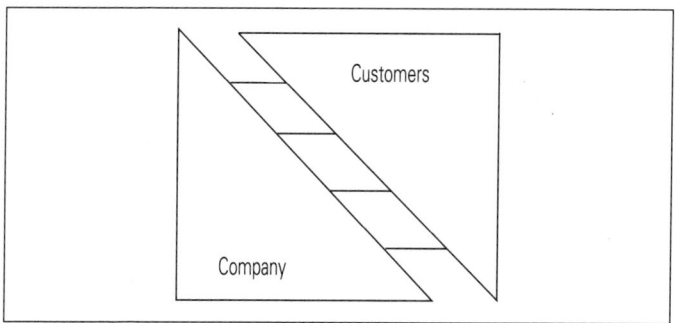

Figure 1. What Is a Business?

company dies. The customer is a person to be served. A friend. A partner in a marriage. This is one of the key ideas upon which TQM is based.

TQM companies put customers on the board of directors and on internal planning committees. They reach out to the customer. They contact the customer, listen to the customer, and accept guidance from the customer. They solicit and act on suggestions and ideas. A good litmus test is to ask whether your company does these things.

Something very extraordinary happens when a customer buys a product or service. Both the *customer* and the *company* profit. By having bought a product or service, the customer now has something that to them is worth more than the money spent for it. This is, of course, why the customer was willing to part with the money in the first place. The company also makes a profit. So both parties are now better off than each was before. It's this magic that makes the business world go round. When the customer loses, that's the beginning of the end. Things get cool. A divorce is in the wind. The marriage is on shaky ground.

COMMUNICATION

As in any marriage, communication is always key. The case of Finning Ltd., the world's largest Caterpillar dealer, illustrates the kind of zeal for customer contact that companies need. Since the firm's outlets are located in small farming communities, employees interact socially with the customers all of the time. When employees pick up complaints, they know what to do with them. They immediately put them into a database that the company has constructed for this purpose. In this way management knows what's going on in the field and can take policy action.[5]

The feedback a company receives from the customer can motivate them to improve or reengineer processes to better meet customer requirements and expectations.

Not actively obtaining such feedback puts a company in a situation of "shooting in the dark." It knows only dimly what to do to satisfy and to keep customers. Instead of keeping the customers it has, it must always find new customers to replace the ones it once had, but failed to satisfy.

THE CUSTOMER-COMPANY-SUPPLIER CHAIN

While the two central parts of a business are the company and the customer, there is usually a need for a third part, the suppliers of basic materials. In manufacturing, suppliers are particularly critical. In some service businesses, like law, they're much less so. In TQM, the idea is to bring suppliers into closer partnership with the company. Make them a real part of the business. Figure 2 shows this chain.

Tying the customer in at one end and the supplier in at the other creates the idea of a customer-producer-supplier chain that forges strong and efficient links. The idea is to be able to trace exact connections backwards, not only from consumers to the manufacturer/producer, but even further — to the suppliers of raw materials and other goods and services that the provider must have.

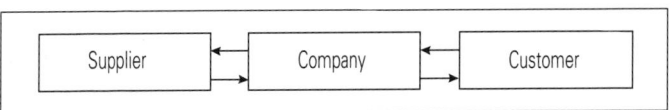

Figure 2. Customer-Company-Supplier Chain

Close interactive communication is imperative. A company may supply the supplier's salespeople with desks and secretarial services while they are on site. Or, a company may even permanently station engineers from the supplier company in their factory or design departments. Executives from the supplier firm may join the board and serve on internal committees. One of the ways in which TQM companies implement this idea is by choosing suppliers on the basis of their ability to supply the company in a reliable, trustworthy, helpful way. Following this, the company brings suppliers into the firm, makes them privy to the firm's problems, and asks them for help.

The supplier in this chain needs the customer feedback information. For example, if the company sells knives that dull too quickly, the supplier, knowing the customer is dissatisfied, might provide the company with a harder steel. A TQM organization makes every attempt to stay close to the supplier and the customer, *actively involving both* as genuine partners. In this way, all actors in the supply chain can work as a team with the one single goal of providing the customer with the ultimate in value.

5
MANAGERIAL ECONOMICS

To a considerable extent, TQM is a business and management paradigm that is concerned with the creation and delivery of maximum economic benefits from scarce and limited resources. The study of how firms do this is called *microeconomics* or, sometimes, *managerial economics*.

ADDING VALUE

Resources may be human, physical, or financial. Sometimes they are in scarce supply, for example, skilled die makers, rare minerals, or venture capital. By applying knowledge and know-how to the use of resources, whether scarce or plentiful, we produce and deliver products or services that have more value to consumers than the resources had before they were put to use. This process is described as *adding value*. A log that has a market value of one hundred dollars may have a value of five hundred after it has been cut and planed into lumber. The cutting and planing have given it an added value of four hundred dollars. If the lumber is transformed into a desk, its value goes up higher still.

The sequence of activities that starts with the felling of the tree and ends with lumber and furniture constitutes an interlinked chain of activities and processes in which value is added at each step. It is referred to as a *value-added* chain. The *inputs* into the process are materials, work, equipment, and finances. The *outputs* are the lumber and furniture. The difference between the market value of the inputs and the market value of the outputs represents the value added by the process. When ways and means are devised to add more value without increasing costs, this ratio improves. An increase in value added takes place. The result can be a better product or service for the customer at a lower price. In addition, the greatly reduced costs can provide a larger margin for the company.

PROCESS IMPROVEMENT

A large part of the cost of producing goods and services is the cost of the *work activities*. Work activities take time. In law, management consulting, engineering, and many other fields the total cost of any project is almost entirely the cost of human time. And, as the old saw puts it, "time is money." Eliminating a work activity eliminates a cost. Simplifying an activity reduces a cost. Most industrial economists, industrial engineers, and managers themselves believe that any organization can eliminate or greatly reduce fifty percent or more of its work activity.

Part of the strategy for achieving these savings (and making things move faster) is to work on a whole process rather than just one activity at a time. For example, some of the processes in the restaurant business are purchasing food, cooking food, and serving food. Each of these processes consists of a number of activities or steps. A restaurant might single out one of these processes because it needs or invites substantial improvement. They then improve the process by eliminating, simplifying, or rearranging the constituent activities.

This procedure is referred to as *process improvement* or *process reengineering*. Using energy and intelligence to reengineer continuously (continuous improvement), a company can make great advances. For example, University of Michigan Hospitals cut the time it takes to admit patients from 2.3 hours to 11 minutes.

ACTIVITY-BASED ACCOUNTING

One of the tools that is helpful in TQM is *activity-based accounting*. This method of accounting establishes the true cost of a service or product by identifying the costs of some or all the work activities that go into the value-added chain, rather than by allocating overhead costs in the traditional manner. It's also known as activity-based costing (ABC). The accounting department must provide the activity-based cost data that TQM process improvement, business reengineering, and decision-making require.[6]

FLOWCHARTS

The flowchart is one of the simplest and most powerful of all the ideas used in TQM. A flowchart can describe any process, from sending a valentine to purchasing a ship. It is a graphic representation of the sequence of activities in a process. It enables one to spot missing, unnecessary, and repetitive steps and make improvements. It also makes it easier to imagine and invent a faster, cheaper, better process, that is, to reengineer processes on a larger scale (business reengineering). The term *imagineering* is sometimes used to emphasize that reengineering is as much a creative process as an analytical one.

Flowcharts make it easier to see where you can eliminate steps and activities or substitute new ones. This saves time and speeds things up. The newly engineered process not only reduces cycle time but also reduces the labor-hours required to provide the output. Reducing labor-hours reduces cost. The result is that the customer gets the product or service faster and at a lower price.

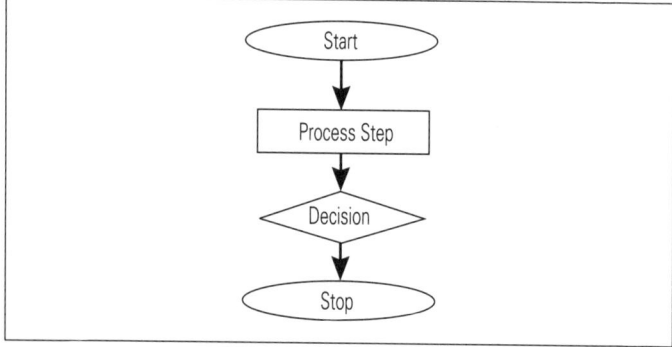

Figure 3. Standard Flowchart Symbols

Flowcharting (or *charting the flow of work*) uses several symbols as conventions to represent process steps. Ovals represent the first and last steps (activities) of a process. Boxes show the in-between activities that take place in the process. Diamonds show decisions that may lead to an optional step or activity or a return to a previous activity. Arrows indicate the direction of flow from one activity to another. Figure 3 shows these standard symbols and their relationships.

BUSINESS REENGINEERING

One of the most impressive applications of TQM is business engineering and business reengineering. This process maps the entire flow of business operations (not just a single process) in detail, from the very furthest supplier, to the producers own processes and operations, to the consumer's purchase, and use of the product.

The engineering process must address the total system. The purpose of the design is to arrange things and processes geographically, physically, technologically, logistically, financially, and in every other way that results in low-cost, high value-added, fast, and responsive delivery of products and services.

Reengineering implies that the whole system was not originally well designed. Through reengineering a company transforms a system into the best possible approximation of what it ideally ought to have been in the first place.

6

TIME-BASED MANAGEMENT

Human time is an economic resource that businesses buy or sell. Time is expensive. The cost of making and delivering products or services is largely the cost of people's time. People are paid for their time by the hour, day, month, or year. A large portion of the corporate budget is allocated to purchasing human time in the form of annual, weekly, daily, or hourly wages and salaries.

A company must strategically deploy and efficiently employ this purchased pool of human time in ways that are cost-effective. TQM firms search endlessly for ways of doing things that take as little time as possible. The effective and efficient management of the corporate time resource is one of the major skills of the TQM executive.

In production, for example, time-based management includes such methodologies as *just-in-time-manufacturing*, which allows a company to manufacture products when the customer needs them, rather than beforehand.

THE CUSTOMER'S TIME

Consumers want the time they spend buying to be pleasant and enjoyable. They certainly don't want the seller to give them a bad time! People hate waiting in line, spending time in unpleasant surroundings, spending time uncomfortably, or spending time being bored.

Consumer-focused companies go through hoops in order to make every minute customers spend with them an enjoyable minute. Ten minutes spent waiting in a line feels ten times as long as ten minutes doing such enjoyable things as chatting with a friend or watching a good movie. Some banks provide television programs for customers to watch while they wait in line. Some provide pleasant music and an elegant decor. The Toronto Dominion Bank pays its customers five dollars if they have to wait in line more than five minutes!

Many products such as dishwashers, frozen meals, and numerous others were created simply to save people from spending time doing things they either don't have time to do or don't like doing. The market for timesaving and time-enhancing products and services is immense and growing.

THE EMPLOYEE'S TIME

The TQM company's heightened consciousness of the social, human, and economic importance of time has led to an increase in the use of such old and new employee relations policies and practices as rest breaks, happy hours, flexible hours, job-sharing, worksharing, shortened work weeks, compassionate leave, sabbatical leave, and variable retirement.

TIME MANAGEMENT SKILLS

Managing time includes developing personal skill for reducing and eliminating routine activities that are not worth the time and replacing them with valuable, high-payoff, creative activities that are maximally rewarding. Here are some examples of low-payoff, *low-quality* time:
- doing things that others could do for you
- reading useless reports

- supervising people too closely

Here are some examples of high-payoff, *high-quality*, uses of time:

- calisthenics
- learning
- human relationships
- creative thinking
- planning
- creating value
- communicating
- motivating

The distinction between high-payoff time and low-payoff time is a key concept in time-based management.

CYCLE TIME

The TQM firm has a fast response time. The cycle time between ordering a hamburger and receiving it at a fast food drive-in has been reduced to very few minutes. The cycle time between ordering a pizza by phone and receiving it at the door has been reduced to thirty minutes or less. Cycle time is the time interval that elapses between the initiation of a business action and its completion.

Cycle time reduction is necessary for several reasons:

- Consumers are more pressed for time than ever before in human history. Waiting is a luxury we can't afford. Firms have to get new products and services to the market faster than ever before, initially to keep up with fast-moving competitors, and then to be ahead of them. This is *time-based competition*.

- Reduced cycle time reduces the costs of products and services because it reduces the amount of time — (labor-hours) it takes to design, produce, or deliver them. This, in turn, results in lower prices and increased sales.

- The net outcome of cycle time reduction is products and services that are *better, cheaper and faster*. This is the name of today's competitive business game. In the process of working to reduce cycle time, a company can simultaneously make improvements in other aspects of the quality of the product and service.

The results of cycle-time reduction are gratifying. Johnson and Johnson reduced the time it takes to develop customized retail displays for chain drugstores and supermarkets from three or four months to thirty days. Motorola used to take eleven days to close its books each month. Now it takes two days.[7]

TIME FLIES

The TQM company is acutely aware that it exists in a world where time flies by at a faster and faster rate, and things change daily. Time is contracting. Some things that once took a lot of time now take no time at all. For example, a faxed letter to Seattle from St. John's takes 15 seconds instead of the week it would take by normal mail ("snail mail"). Human life, which was once only a few decades long, now begins to approach a century in length. Time has acquired a whole new set of meanings and dimensions. It has moved to front and center of the business stage. It's a major challenge that the TQM manager has to recognize and deal with.

7
THE SYSTEMS CONCEPT

The systems concept is one of the governing ideas behind TQM. It encourages us to figure out how the several parts of anything fit together to form one integrated, unitary whole. It then enables us to figure out how to make the parts mesh together better so that the system as a whole functions better.

Systems thinking led us to realize that both customers and suppliers are intrinsic parts of a business. A business works best when the links between these various parts of the business are close and function in an integrated and coordinated way. Strengthening the links in the value-added chain that connects suppliers, producers, and customers is one of the important things that happen when the systems idea is taken to heart.

THE SOCIOECONOMIC SYSTEM

The systems concept also invites us to think more strategically by recognizing the extent to which the welfare of a business is determined by how well it fits itself into the surrounding economic system and all of its technological and social dynamics. Systems thinking leads top management to see the firm as an *open*, intimate, and interactive part of the larger, dynamically changing society and economy. It is seen as a part of the whole, rather than an isolated island.

SYSTEMS, CONNECTIONS, AND SUBSYSTEMS

Systems thinking occurs when we become conscious of the systems nature of reality and learn to see systems and interconnections everywhere. What's a system? The human body with its different parts and processes is one example of a system. So is a flower, a tree, or a lake. An automobile is a system, and so is a computer, a computer network, or a robot. Likewise a family, a corporation, or a country is a system. The whole universe and everything in it is constructed of systems that range in size and in hierarchical order from the smallest atom to the largest galaxy.

Parts are systems in their own right—subsystems of the larger system. Take the heart as an example. The heart is part of the circulatory system. But it is also a system itself. It consists of muscles, valves, nerves, and other components that all have to function in exact coordination. The general rule is that every system is composed of subsystems and is itself part of a larger system. Defining systems and their connectivities is a key to understanding them and managing them.

THINKING HOLISTICALLY

Systems thinkers always keep in mind that *the whole is more than and different from the sum of its parts*. For example, water is something more than and different from the hydrogen and oxygen that compose it; it has all sorts of properties and attributes that neither hydrogen nor oxygen themselves possess. We do not grasp a flower's beauty simply by describing its petals, stamen, and other parts. Describing all the departments of IBM one by one doesn't describe IBM the company.

Systems thinking contrasts with analytical thinking, which looks only at the separate parts. TQM says that improving one part of the business while neglecting the others doesn't work. And fixing them all separately doesn't work either. Everything has to be made to fit together.

LIVING SYSTEMS

Living systems, such as human bodies or business enterprises, have some special features. They keep themselves integrated, directed, and in balance by subsystems of communication and control. They are self-managing and dynamic. In dynamic systems, continuous self-adjustment occurs through information feedback and control. A human body automatically develops a tan to protect itself from the sun's rays. A company losing money almost certainly starts to cut back on waste and looks for ways of doing more with less (productivity improvement).

INTEGRATION AND COORDINATION

Systems thinking looks at the forest as well as the trees. Systems thinkers see the business as a complex system whose constituent subsystems—people, technology, money, management processes—have to mesh together. Managers who are systems thinkers attach high value to integration and coordination.

In non-TQM companies, the separate departments often act as if they were in business to advance their own interest rather than the interests of the next guy who ought, in fact, to be regarded as a customer. Such departments have often been compared to missile silos encased in barriers of impenetrable concrete, bristling with armaments, and impervious to outsiders.

In TQM companies the departments collaborate to help one another, advance the common good, and to serve their ultimate partner, the customer. Multi-departmental, cross-functional teams are the main mechanisms that TQM uses for this purpose. The teams turn the hard silos into porous sand. They work through collaborative action, which is turned toward the common cause.

THE HUMAN-MACHINE INTERFACE

In TQM, people and machines work in a symbiotic relationship: the machines complement the work of people and people complement the work of machines. This human-machine relationship is a *sociotechnical system*, that, if properly designed can be described as a *high-performance work system*.

THE STAKEHOLDER IDEA

The idea that a business is a system with several important different parts leads to other ideas. The other ideas address the legal and moral rights of the people who make up the other parts. The rights of the shareholders are well established — they own the *company*. But the *business* consists of much more than the company. TQM respects the rights and interests of *all stakeholders*: employees, customers, and suppliers as well as owners and executives. This bonds them all into a single synergistic whole that is united by common visions, values, commitments, and goals. The idea is for all to be winners. The stakeholder concept is another example of systems thinking.

Research shows that keeping the interests of all the stakeholders firmly in mind pays off in better bottom-line results. Professors Max Clarkson, Michael C. Deck, and their colleagues at the Center for Corporate Social Performance and Ethics at the University of Toronto reported that "...in order to achieve average or above average profits in its industry, a corporation must manage its stakeholder relationships in order to satisfy the needs and expectations of its principal stakeholder groups on a continuing basis. Without such balanced performance the data showed that

32 THE TQM PARADIGM

Figure 4. Partners and Stakeholders

corporations did not achieve above-average profits in their industries."

A stakeholder group is any group that has a vested interest in the survival and success of a business enterprise or any other organization. The group may not own stock but it does have a *stake* in the business.

What are the legitimate interests and rights of the other parts of the business as a total system (the customers, the suppliers, the community)? Does that stake give them certain rights? The law often says so. Stakeholders' rights are increasingly being written into the law and are receiving increasing legal protection. Legislation already exists in over twenty-five U.S. states that ordains that the Board of Directors has a responsibility to *all* stakeholders.

8

MANAGEMENT

The third of the three main ideas in TQM is the management process—the governing process through which a company achieves quality and excellence. The management process is not a new idea, but it is certainly one of the most important ideas contained in TQM. It provides the framework within which TQM operates. The objective of the management process is to produce quality *results*.

DISCOVERY OF THE MANAGEMENT PROCESS

The existence of a management process was first discovered by the French executive, Henri Fayol, around 1890. He was looking for an explanation as to why some firms were successful and others were failures, even when both had equally good products and financing and equally good market opportunities. So he began to look into what went on in the two types of firms.

He discovered that firms that survived and thrived consciously planned, organized, coordinated, communicated, implemented and controlled things. By control, Fayol meant monitoring what was going on, seeing if the right results were produced, and taking corrective action to ensure that they would be. This sequence of activities that Fayol uncovered has since come to be referred to as the management process. In contrast, firms that failed—the majority—did not engage in any such process. Eventually, they went bankrupt. To Fayol, this was a big *Eureka* — he had found his answer. For Fayol the discovery became a mission. He pushed the idea of the management process in books and speeches. He urged governments and government departments, schools, hospitals, and other public sector institutions to use it.

Slowly but surely, Fayol's idea spread. In 1921, General Motors rescued itself from imminent bankruptcy by applying the management process to its business. Then, labeling its own version of the management process, "the General Motors Management System," GM went on, under the leadership of Alfred Sloan, to become the largest and most profitable corporation in world history. In 1950, Ralph Cordiner, CEO of General Electric, did for G.E. what Sloan had done for GM. In adopting the management process, G.E. not only saved itself from imminent bankruptcy, but went on to become enormously successful. It called its version of the management process, the "General Electric Management Philosophy."

MANAGEMENT AND TQM

Today, a hundred years after Fayol, leading-edge firms easily recognize the importance and power of the management process. Yet a large number of business organizations still are not aware of this concept and do not employ it. As a result, their quality attempts fail.

We now appreciate that excellence and quality are ideals we must turn into goals and projects that we achieve by planned effort. The *management process* is how we do it. That's why *management* is one of the three main ideas in Total Quality Management.

The TQM company formulates missions, forms visions, expresses goals, develops strategies, assembles and organizes resources, formulates objectives, devises and implements plans, monitors results, and then reexamines and alters the whole process as need be. The TQM company does this in a conscious, deliberate, intelligent way under the leadership of senior executives who know how to do it and how to make things happen by applying the management process.

The successful move toward excellence and quality requires the intense personal commitment of the CEO. TQM represents a change in the traditional corporate culture of most companies and requires the unswerving attention and dedication of the CEO. It also requires a similar dedication from all the other managers. According to their own testimony, creating a TQM culture is one of the greatest challenges to leadership and the management of change that a top executive group will ever encounter.

STRATEGIC MANAGEMENT

Strategic management is the special process of fitting the firm's products, services, and operations effectively into the ever-changing market situation. These days the market is highly global in its character and influence, and highly dynamic, turbulent, and changing.

The idea of strategy comes from the military. But now we know that strategy is essential to success in every human undertaking: sports, politics, business, and every other.

Strategic management depends on the ability to *think strategically*. Strategic thinking entails thinking through such concepts as the business you are in; the shape, form, and direction the market is taking; the core competencies the company possesses; what the future seems to hold; and what we can do to provide the market with the services and products it needs and wants.

People who are good strategists use a combination of logical thinking, penetrating perception, and creative imagination. This often results in what we call *strategic insights*. A strategic insight is a vivid and usually surprising recognition of the strategies that are necessary and that will produce success.

Experience in strategic management reveals that *implementing* a strategy can be a monumentally difficult challenge. For a strategy to produce the required results, we have to both start and carry out the plans and programs successfully. Many strategies fail because we do not recognize the difficulty inherent in implementation. He is also critical for top management to commit to seeing that the implementation takes place effectively. Recent research indicates that too many senior executives neglect this important obligation.[8]

In recent years, Japan has developed hoshin management, a specially crafted version of the strategic management process.[9] *Hoshin* means "a methodology for strategic direction setting." Hoshin management was designed specifically for the management of corporate change and improvement in TQM companies. It has become popular in the United States. Hewlett-Packard, Florida Power & Light, Xerox, and Intel, among others have adopted and adapted it to their own needs. Any company venturing into TQM must become familiar with this strategically masterful methodology.

As a first step in the hoshin process, corporate management identifies factors that are critical to the success of the company. Management studies the environment of the business. The purpose is to discover the specific *challenges of change* the company faces, and the *responses* the company needs to make. Then management determines exactly where the company needs *improvement* if it wants to respond successfully to these challenges. Then, *improvement objectives* are formulated and deployed down through the company by setting specific objectives at each level that will facilitate achieving the over-all company objective.

Hoshin management has a built-in concern for implementing strategy. The system *tracks and monitors* implementation and provides for *corrective action* when the objectives are not met. The hoshin management process also contains a built-in procedure that ensures continuous review of the operation of hoshin itself. The purpose is to continuously improve the operational planning and management of the business, rather than to leave an unquestioned, static management system in place.

JURAN TRILOGY

The Juran trilogy was formulated by Dr. Joseph M. Juran, one of the great pioneers of quality management. It consists of three management processes that he thinks are essential to quality achievement:

1. quality planning
2. quality control
3. quality improvement

As part of the improvement process, Juran advocates the identification of team projects. The idea is that a company can single out the improvements they need to make (those that are in line with corporate strategy) and organize teams to work on these strategically important improvement projects.

PLAN-DO-CHECK-ACT

Managing quality improvement at the operating level is often referred to as *PDCA* or *plan-do-check-act*. This four-step quality management method was developed by Walter A. Shewhart, a statistician in Bell Labs in the 'twenties and 'thirties.

Shewhart also pioneered the use of statistical tools to monitor, measure, and control variations in quality. In

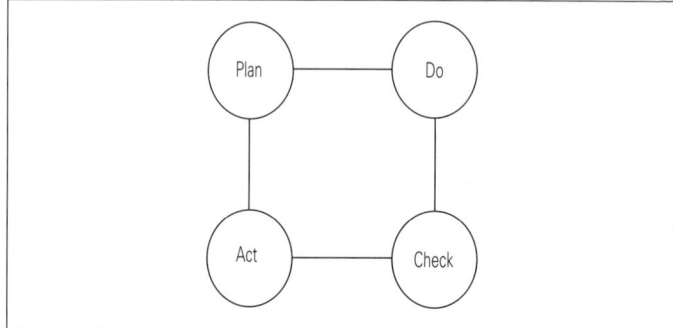

Figure 5. Plan-Do-Check-Act

addition, he pioneered the use of control charts in the "check" part of the process. Today the use of statistical methods, PDCA, and control charts is found everywhere in TQM firms. (See Figure 5.)

SCIENTIFIC MANAGEMENT

TQM's use of measurement, statistics, charts, graphs, and analysis reflects the idea that operations management should be scientific and logical rather than seat-of-the-pants and shoot-from-the-hip. Observation, data, facts, and measurement should replace supposition, guesswork, and opinion.

Mechanical engineers working in factories before the turn of this century were first to bring this idea into business. They saw they could extend the same mathematical and analytical approaches they used to measure and design machinery and its operation to other things. They believed the idea of going about things scientifically could apply to work flow, work processes, work methods, and factory and office layout. The engineers who moved in this direction came to refer to themselves as industrial engineers. Many of the tools and techniques they evolved over subsequent decades are part of quality and productivity work today. Some of their tools that are widely used in TQM today are cause-and-effect diagrams, Pareto charts, and control charts, among many others.

Industrial engineers were also first to work on the questions of productivity and quality. We now apply this scientific, or fact-based mode of thinking, not only in production, but in marketing, public relations, customer service, human resources management, and other areas. For example, rather than assuming or guessing they know what the customer wants, marketing departments in TQM firms do surveys and gather data and facts on what the customer actually does want. They similarly gather data on what customers think and feel about what they are currently getting.

TECHNOLOGY MANAGEMENT

The impact of technology on quality is everywhere. For example, ecologically benign automobiles, powered by hydrogen extracted from lake water, or by power packs in which electricity is generated from aluminum, will offer their developers some strategic marketing advantages. Biotechnology is opening up whole new industries, such as prosthetics, and transforming others, such as agriculture. Gene splicing is resulting in better quality crops and new animals. Genetic engineering is improving the quality of health care. It can treat more and more diseases and disorders.

Along with quality people, quality technology ranks high among the list of factors that make a firm more globally competitive. Modern technology can make a firm more powerful. It helps produce and deliver new and superior products and services. It helps serve markets and customers more effectively. To rank as a high-quality company is to rank high in technology management.

Technology management is emerging as a distinct art and science in its own right in the same sense as financial management, marketing management, or manufacturing management. It's a relatively new idea that embraces R&D and includes organization and deployment of appropriate technologies in manufacturing and warehousing, transportation, marketing, and even in the corporate head office or the accounting department. It's a big concept. TQM firms often have vice presidents of technology management, whose function includes helping the firm make strategic use of every technology possible and desirable and in every phase of the business.

Universities offer special programs that lead to graduate degrees in Technology Management. It is a growing field of scholarly research. Management consulting firms now have technology management divisions that help clients manage technology both strategically and operationally.

Excellence in technology management includes the astute use of high-quality information technologies, ranging from computers, teleconferencing, faxes, satellites, cellular phones, video phones, multimedia, robotics, automation, expert systems, artificial intelligence, to virtual reality and more to come.

In TQM firms, technology has a human face. Everyone is given maximum training and support in the use of new technologies and participates in the selection and/or design of technologies.

DIONYSIAN MANAGEMENT

Dionysian management is an idea that contrasts with and complements scientific management. TQM firms that get it right usually marry the scientific and the Dionysian spirits in a productive union.

TQM endorses the Dionysian approach, which is an exuberant, energetic, adventuresome, risk-taking, spirited, creative, and entrepreneurial approach to business. Jack Welch, the charismatic leader of G.E., speaks for the Dionysian spirit when he says his company can survive only if it can fully release the emotional energies of all its members.

The Dionysian firm encourages the generation of ideas, imagination, invention, and innovation. The Dionysian spirit advocates outspoken humor and joking in the workplace. It favors camaraderie, celebrations, reunions, and Friday afternoon fun breaks. It promotes the use of art and color on office and factory walls. It takes symbols, rituals, and customs seriously. It wants the workplace to be human.

The scientific management approach takes advantage of the human ability to apply logic and reason to data and facts. The Dionysian approach takes advantage of the emotional and spiritual ability of the human to go beyond the facts, open new horizons, act boldly, demonstrate courage and conviction, and create a better world.

QUALITY MANAGEMENT

The phrase "quality management" has two meanings, depending on which of the two words you emphasize. One meaning is the commonly understood management of quality. The other meaning is *the quality of management*. We can pronounce it *quality* management as we usually do. But we can also pronounce it quality *management*. Try it and see. The distinction is extremely important. Why? Because the quality of management in a firm determines whether TQM will work. An excellent example is provided by Federal Express. John Slangerup, general manager of Federal Express's Canadian division, expresses it emphatically when he talks about what it takes to deliver total customer satisfaction. He says that ability *lives and dies by the quality of managers.* In Federal Express, as in other TQM firms, achieving the necessary level of quality in management requires an intense training and development of managers that goes far beyond what we normally find in business.

9

BUSINESS IS PEOPLE

The TQM idea that business is people and that everything must center on this realization is not as trite as it sounds. TQM says that ethical and human values come first. When everyone in business treats everyone else with respect and trust everyone is better off.

Since a business transaction is always a transaction between human beings, it is an error in logical thinking to regard customers as numbers, dollars, and statistics. It is more logical to think always of customers as human beings who think, feel, and act. Human beings' actions can make or break a business. Inside the company itself, interactions are not between "employees" and "managers", but between people. These interactions constitute a large, complex, collaborative process.

EMPLOYEES AS MANAGERS AND ENTREPRENEURS

In the old days, managers expected employees to do what they were told, in the way they were told. In the new world of TQM the employee is expected to think, feel, and act as a manager. They become self-managing and semi-autonomous in the same way managers are.

The art and practice of management — good management — is one of the key concepts in Total Quality Management. In TQM companies, everyone from top to bottom knows how to use the management process to achieve the goals of the enterprise. Management is a definite skill that everyone consciously employs. (In some TQM firms, the term "employee" has been dropped as inappropriate. After all, managers too are employees of the firm. The classical terminology has never made sense. Managers and employees alike are equally "members" of the firm.)

In TQM every employee is also an entrepreneur for the organization. We can call them *intrapreneurs*. Every person in the organization is in business for himself or herself. As with all businesses, their purpose is to serve their customers. These customers include bosses, reports, and peers, as well as the ultimate customer. A TQM company measures success by the degree to which you help other people perform their function better and how you perform your own. This is fundamental to the personal work ethic in the TQM organization. The quality of the people in the TQM firm is measured by their ability to do just that. It's a big part of the TQM idea.

In the TQM organization, employees are more autonomous. They set their own goals in line with the corporate mission and their unit's purpose. They are assertive and proactive rather than passive and reactive. They do not work mechanically and prescriptively from the classical cut-and-dried job description. Job descriptions are out. Instead, everyone receives a brief role statement. The role statement provides only an essential frame of reference. Nothing more. That's all an intrapreneur needs.

Intrapreneurial employees take the initiative. They respond to the challenges and opportunities around them. They focus less on doing tasks per se and more on producing outcomes that add value. They have highly developed intraprenurial, proactive, performance skills. Thus they are equipped to serve their existing organization and to sell their services to future employers. In a world of change and transience, that day will always come.

THEORY X AND THEORY Y

The idea underlying intrapreneurship and self-management is known as Theory Y. The term was coined in the late 'forties by Professor Douglas McGregor of MIT. Theory Y says that most people, employees and managers alike, want responsibility, want to collaborate with their fellows, and want to exercise initiative and creativity. Some executives, often senior executives, are Theory Y believers. It is self-evident to them that employees will take readily to teamwork, empowerment, improvement programs, creative thinking, process reengineering, goal-setting, and self-management. Theory Y managers believe that they should act as leaders, mentors, coaches, trainers, and assistants to their subordinates.

Some executives, however, are Theory X types, McGregor noted. Theory X types have the opposite idea about human nature. They believe that employees are inherently lazy, irresponsible, lacking in initiative, and incapable of intelligent and creative thought. Theory X managers believe they have to closely supervise and control employees. They believe employees will work conscientiously only if they receive the promise of rewards or the threat of penalties. Theory X companies even handle managers, up to the vice-president level, in a similar way.

Historically, most companies have been of the Theory X persuasion. They want managers to give orders and directions, supervise and monitor their subordinates, praise and reward them for doing what's wanted, and criticize and penalize them for failing.

When companies manage in a Theory X style, employees do not demonstrate initiative. They do not seek responsibility. They do not think up new things to do or better ways of doing things. They look out mainly for themselves. The Theory X executives, who created this dismal state of affairs, use it as proof that they were right about people all along!

In Theory Y companies, the opposite thing happens. Employees demonstrate initiative, seek responsibility, make decisions, produce clever and practical new ideas, continuously improve things, and help the other guy when needed. Theory Y executives also take this state of affairs as proof that they were right about people all along.

What it seems to boil down to is that Theory X managers bring out the worst in people and Theory Y managers bring out the best.

Theory X companies are restricted to the traditional authoritarian approaches to quality. They base quality control on inspection by specialized quality departments, and handle failures to comply with threat and coercion. As its customer service strategy, a Theory X pizza company in Toronto threatened its delivery people with fines and dismissal if they were caught not smiling while handing the pizza to the customer.

TQM firms are Theory Y to the limit. In some instances, employee teams manage themselves to the point of performing such managerial functions as dividing their work up as they see fit. They may order their own materials and supplies. They themselves may actually hire new team members. They may be empowered to deal directly, and at their own discretion, with customers and staff departments without going through their supervisors. Individual employees are also empowered to make autonomous decisions. In the Ritz-Carlton hotel chain, for example, if a guest complains about a room any employee is empowered to get the guest another room. Ultimately the traditional term, "employee," seems inappropriate. TQM companies may replace it with a more descriptive word, such as "associate," or "partner."

TOTAL INVOLVEMENT

The TQM company is *people-centered and participatory. Human will, brains, energy, and passion* drive it. It is *collaborative and cooperative*. Total involvement is a hallmark of the TQM philosophy. It involves the mind and the heart; it is emotional as well as mental. It produces a company that is truly committed to excellence in all things.

Every person, from top to bottom, gets involved and committed. The Board of Directors, the CEO, the top-management team — all are involved. The shipping clerk, the buyer, the factory worker, the accounting clerk, and the sales representative are involved. The suppliers and the customers, as well as the company are involved. No longer are quality assurance and quality control people the only ones seriously involved. The CEO, however, is the one most involved through his or her constant effort to inspire, lead, and support the whole quality effort. If CEOs are not dedicated to the quality effort, employees won't be either.

LEARNING

In the TQM enterprise, employees receive substantial amounts of training, education, and coaching in order to function confidently at higher levels of authority and responsibility. The amount of training needed is a great deal more than is customary in the traditional "just-do-as-you're-told" organizations of the pre-TQM era. Ten days per year (annually) is a likely rule-of-thumb.

Learning and empowerment go hand in hand. Knowledge is power. When the abilities, skills, and knowledge of an entire organization rise to a new and higher position of power, that organization itself gains enormously in strength.

Organizations that use learning as a strategy for survival and success represent a new wave. The new wave is especially appropriate in the new type of economy that has emerged. It is an economy based on products or services that are knowledge-intensive.

A knowledge-intensive business is one in which values are added. It is created mainly by using and applying knowledge rather than materials. For example, a desktop computer contains only a few pounds of metal, plastic, and silicon, but it contains an amount of knowledge that took billions of dollars worth of research and development to produce. It is adding this knowledge to the few pounds of materials that gives the computer its value.

In a TQM firm, workers apply their creativity and their knowledge of problem solving, and improvement methodologies to the challenge of finding better, more cost-effective, and higher-quality ways of doing things. The use of knowledge for business purposes has become a permanent part of the new economy. Consequently, learning, the avenue through which knowledge is acquired, is critical to survival and success.

The Learning Organization

We now realize that individuals in the organization need to engage in lifelong learning. We have also realized that the organization itself must continuously learn how to manage itself better and better. It must learn more about its environment and keep this knowledge current. It must learn more about its competitors. It must constantly learn and relearn what the business environment tells it. It must learn ever better ways of marketing, research, manufacturing, public relations, human relations, accounting, finance, and so on. The TQM company must learn which strategies work, and which don't. The company that doesn't learn and relearn fast these days will be sunk by competitors that do.

Action Learning

Often the most valuable things that people learn come not only from books and courses, but from experience and action. Napoleon put it this way: "First I act, then I find out." Action learning entails trial and error. Each time someone makes an error or discovers a mistake, he or she (and the company) knows more about what not to do. They don't repeat the mistake. The next action may be the right one. If not, eventually they'll discover the right thing to do. And they'll use this right way until a better way is found. They'll find a better way through still more trials and still more mistakes. There is no end to the advances and improvements a company and its people can make again and again through learning by trial and error.

Paradoxically it turns out that humans (and other creatures) often learn best by doing things wrong! Mistakes are golden. James Bere, Chairman of Borg Warner, puts it this way: "Most people do not want to take the risk of failure, and therefore they do not want their people to make mistakes. And I say it's the absolute reverse. You do not develop a quality person without making mistakes."[10]

Team Learning

TQM makes great use of team learning in which teams carry out their own learning activities rather than being taught by an instructor. Team learning has also been called synergogy, which means learning together.[11]

Synergogy

- replaces authority figures with learning designs and instruments that a learning administrator manages.

- enables learners to become proactive participants who exercise responsibility for their own learning. The teamwork atmosphere provides motivation for learning. Synergogy also brings about synergy. The learning gain that results from teamwork thus exceeds the gain the individual makes by learning alone.

TEAMS AND TEAMWORK

TQM employs *teams and teamwork* from top to bottom in an organization and from left to right across it. The network of teams that operate in such firms is sometimes extensive enough to be referred to as a *parallel organization*. In particular, the use of cross-departmental teams can integrate and improve the logical flow and quality of value-adding processes involved in the design, production, and delivery of the product or service.

That it's a good idea to do things in teams, whether in the executive suite or the shop floor, is new to the business world. Previously, business focused all responsibility in the hands of individuals. The status quo was that individuals worked separately on their own part of the job. In North America, with its long tradition of individualism, the idea of teams and teamwork rarely entered the minds of managers. In some cases, companies regarded it as a politically incorrect idea that threatened important moral values. It is hard to realize that in such a short time an idea that was previously derided is now held in such regard.

LEADERS AND LEADERSHIP

Because the TQM paradigm focuses on people, managers do not function only in the traditional Fayolian pattern of planning, organizing, implementing and controlling operations. They also act as leaders. Leaders look ahead, keep ahead, and move ahead. They are always at the forefront. They're in the vanguard of events. They are proactive and make things happen. They guide, support, inspire, assist, and empower those who report to them. And they do it with feeling, from the heart.

TQM carries the leadership concept even further. In TQM everybody—employee and manager alike—is expected to exercise leadership whenever the situation is appropriate. In particular, since TQM relies heavily on Improvement Teams, Project Teams, and Innovation Teams, *team leadership skills* become part of everyone's training.

Within the TQM culture, every employee is a manager as well as a leader. Each individual has a particular zone of responsibility to manage. Everyone learns how to use the management process. Texas Instruments has been training employees how to use the management process and to be self-managing for thirty or more years. The rest of the world is finally catching up with paradigm-breaking pioneers like TI.

Finally, TQM companies encourage every manager and employee to be entrepreneurial. They ask them to be creative, enterprising and innovative; to take risks and make mistakes. They teach them how to function in this entrepreneurial mode and reward them for doing so.

THREE DIMENSIONS

The new three-dimensional role—manager, leader, entrepreneur—demands a lot from people: vision, dedication, courage, compassion, fortitude, and imagination. These roles transcend what is traditionally expected from those who function only in the classical plan-and-control mode.

Nothing is more essential to TQM than having people aboard who crave to become everything of which they are innately capable. TQM calls out and employs the qualities that make humans truly human. It's an ambitious goal, but then, TQM is an ambitious idea.

TQM increases the spirit of teamwork among the members of the enterprise, and the company, and between suppliers, the company, and its customers. It emphasizes a *lateral* or *horizontal* form of human interaction that links suppliers, company members, and customers into *a single value-adding chain*. It eliminates, or at least minimizes, hierarchy. As a result, fewer intermediaries between the top and bottom levels are necessary. Several organizational levels disappear from the middle. The organization is now flat rather than tall. It looks more like a baseball diamond than a pyramid.

10

HYPERCHANGE

Change can be incremental (a snail crossing a road) or transformational (caterpillar into butterfly). It can be slow or fast, linear or exponential, superficial or deep, gradual or abrupt, creative or destructive, desirable or undesirable, predictable or unpredictable, planned or accidental (serendipitous). But change can also be so radical and encompassing that we can call it *hyperchange*. Hyperchange involves technology, society, culture, politics, and even our mental states.

The four types of changes that characterize hyperchange are:

- slow, evolutionary change
- exponential change
- discontinuous change
- randomly unpredictable change

Random and unpredictable change is occurring more and more frequently, often with violent impact. It is the most volatile component of hyperchange.

Hyperchange is here to stay and we need to adopt a wholly new paradigm for management. The TQM style of management is designed for survival and success in this economic environment of hyperchange.

The new TQM management paradigm has six distinguishing features. TQM is:

- outward looking
- change responsive
- future focused
- people centered
- idea driven
- creative and innovative

OUTWARD LOOKING

A TQM company views itself as part of the larger planetary whole that is made up of the local state, the nation, the community of trading blocks, and developed and developing countries. It is not self-centered, nor an island unto itself. It both depends upon its environment and serves it.

So TQM management constantly searches, scans, and explores the environment on a global scale. It establishes more ties and closer ties with the community and the consumer, with suppliers and governments, and with other firms in its own and allied industries. Rather than being isolated and alone a TQM company seeks out and creates webs and networks of interconnections and mutual support not only in the business sector, but in the public sector.

Social responsibility is a strong feature of the TQM company, as is ecological consciousness and a strong business ethic.

Its outward-looking character is supported by appropriate goals, strategies, and programs in marketing, government relations, community relations, and public responsibility.

CHANGE RESPONSIVE

TQM organizations themselves engage in a life of perpetual change. Their triple purpose is to:

1. survive and thrive by adapting to change
2. take advantage of the new opportunities that change provides
3. create change in the marketplace through creativity and innovation

The new management is change-responsive, change-seeking, and change-making. It not only adapts to change and its complexities and ambiguities, it welcomes change. It views change as a source of opportunity as well as threat. It adopts a positive attitude toward change.

The new management creates a corporate culture that encourages change. It teaches employees how to create change. It stays alert to detect in the outer environment both changes that are threats and changes that are opportunities. While it always takes steps to deal with threats, it puts its main energy into changes that open up new opportunities. Some speak of the *markets of change*.

A company's role is also to initiate changes that benefit its own customers and the economy as a whole. The TQM company ceaselessly alters, transforms, and reinvents itself. As it continuously improves and develops, the TQM company is in a permanent state of transition and changes day by day.

Individuals in today's cauldron of hyperchange need to support one another, keep fit, move fast, develop skills in stress management, and learn how to employ ingenuity and imagination. Companies need to train their people in these new survival, health management, and performance abilities.

FUTURE FOCUS

We divide time into past, present, and future. In a world where time flies faster than ever before, the TQM company senses that the future is upon us before we know it. Today quickly becomes yesterday. The past is over and done with. The questions always are: What comes next? What does next week hold, or next month, next year, the next ten or twenty years?

The idea is that we are time travelers, like or not, and the trip moves fast. It's a new idea. We never thought of it that way in the past. We don't need the time machine imagined by H.G. Wells. The whole world moves ahead and we move with it. We're already headed quickly into the future — faster than we may want.

The TQM firm constantly looks ahead, anticipating what it will do next and what it can eventually become. Does the future hold growth and progress or stagnation, decay, and bankruptcy? We can't do anything about the past, and only a little about the present, but we can do a great deal about the future.

TQM companies use vision and imagination to create pictures in the mind of alternative possible futures. We already know many features of the future. There will be more telecommunication facilities and technologies, a larger world population, many new medical breakthroughs, and an aging population.

How do those futures translate into opportunities for our own company or ourselves? The future also holds many surprises for us. Just think of what's been happening in Russia that no one expected. Think of how the world was so suddenly presented with the fax, the cellular phone, and the home computer. The future-focused firm organizes for surprises, good and bad. It stays loose and flexible and keeps its eyes and ears open.

11

IDEA GENERATION

Visions, concepts, ideas, thought, and creativity drive the new management. It knows that the new world unfolding before our eyes is the product of the human brain and spirit and of its logical, constructive, and inventive capabilities. These capabilities have brought and will continue to bring us new products, new services, new forms of commercial organization, new social institutions , and new political and economic arrangements. The new management puts to work the best available scientific knowledge about the human brain and mind and how we can help it work better. This knowledge is about problem solving, observation, analysis, vision, planning, goal-setting, intuition, imagination, and creativity.

TQM teaches people how to get and use information and knowledge. It promotes ceaseless learning at the individual, group, and organizational level. TQM taps the deeper levels of human intelligence — our understanding and wisdom. This deeper tapping ensures that the human mind and will put the power of information and knowledge to intelligent and constructive use.

The new managers create a corporate climate that encourages us to challenge the status quo. Members of the company develop irreverent attitudes toward existing ideas and practices. This encourages fresh thinking, imaginative ideas, and new solutions.

TQM managers, such as those at GM, encourage the use of *creativity teams*, which challenge and rethink existing practices and conventions. They encourage the use of *innovation teams*, which are set up to invent and innovate new products, services, or administrative arrangements in every field of the business. They teach everyone how to think creatively and how to use some of the available techniques.

Using brainpower, through thought and attention, we can discover and implement steady, daily, small changes and improvements. They may not make much difference from one day to another but they add up to big changes over a period of time. A daily improvement of one percent compounds to over a hundred percent improvement in only three months. But imagination and creativity can help us also make quantum leaps in quality and value as well as slow and steady gains. Increasingly, global competition requires both the incremental and the quantum leap strategies.

Yes, steady incremental improvements can produce big results. But the results from quantum jumps are bigger still. Creative thinking, and the competitive advantage it provides, moves us ahead by leaps and bounds.

CREATIVE THINKING TECHNIQUES

TQM companies train everyone, from CEO to janitor, in the techniques that develop creative thinking. These techniques combine the use of quantitative analytical thinking of the scientific management school with the intuitive and imaginative thinking of the Dionysian school. The purpose is to come up with breakthrough ideas. Some ideas may be at a micro level, such as improvements in machine shop practice. Other ideas can be at the macro level, such as new strategic approaches to global markets.

For some years, General Foods Canada operated an "Idea Center" where creativity teams were trained in methods of divergent and unorthodox thinking. Then they worked on such projects as inventing new ways of packaging coffee, displaying cereals, or training customers. The teams met in a specially designed facility with off-beat decor, where relaxing music played gently in the background, and where floor-to-ceiling windows opened out on a long vista of trees and hills. Eventually creative team thinking became such a habit that a formal center was no longer necessary.

A description of a few of the many available creativity techniques follows.[12]

Bioheuristics

Bioheuristics (originally called bionics) is a method for finding solutions to business problems (from finance to design) by finding out how organisms (from bacteria to elephants) deal with problems in their own domain. When the researchers find a solution in the world of organisms, they minutely examine it, then copy and adapt it to the business world.

Everyone has a piece of clothing, or luggage, or something that closes with Velcro fasteners. Velcro was a successful attempt to imitate the structure of burrs — those annoying little objects that catch onto your dog's fur. Burrs work with tiny hooks that grab, stick, and cling tenaciously. So does Velcro. Velcro is merely one example of the many ideas we have borrowed from nature.

Over the ages, bioheuristics has led us to make pliers that resemble the lobster's claw, fishnets that resemble the spider's web, traps that resemble the Venus's flytrap's machinations, and airplanes that resemble birds. An interesting twist is the navy's F118, which has legs that imitate those of the grasshopper in order to ease the shock of carrier landing. Camouflage techniques drawn from animal and plant life are other examples of bioheuristics.

To use bioheuristics, follow these steps:

1. Clarify what the problem is.
2. Think of plants, animals, or other organisms that have solutions to this type of problem.
3. Pick the one that seems most interesting.
4. Examine it in minute detail, and use a specimen if possible.
5. Figure out whether you can copy, imitate, or emulate its solution.

Concept Displacement

Concept displacement takes an idea from one field and applies it to another. For example, in the theater, people act out, or play various roles in a play. Role-playing has become useful in other settings for other purposes. Some psychotherapists ask their patients to act out various roles that can help the therapist and the patient get more insight into the patient's behavioral problems. In another and different context, industrial trainers ask sales trainees to act out imaginary selling situations so that they can observe, analyze, and improve their sales behavior. Sometimes trainers use video cameras to help the trainee look at what has happened.

Creative Contradiction

Creative contradiction makes use of opposites. Sometimes we can find a creative solution by doing the opposite of what seems logical or what is customary. At other times, we find the solution by combining a customary or orthodox answer with its opposite in order to create a synthesis of the two.

The glass window was invented to do two contradictory things: let light in but keep air out. The shutter, in contrast, was invented to let air in but keep light out! The common rubber-tipped pencil was invented so that we could do either of two opposite things: put words on paper or take them off.

You do it this way:

1. List the current solution in use (for example, appraising exployees.)

2. List its opposite (for example, appraising managers.)

3. Figure out how to do both at the same time (for example, create a system where managers and employees appraise how well they work together.)

Morphology

Morphology is a technique that uses a three-dimensional grid. Each dimension represents one aspect of a business design problem and is broken down into a number of elements. We construct trial designs by choosing random elements from each dimension. For example, what new products could your firm make using what materials for what people?

The method was invented by Fritz Zwicky, a brilliantly successful and totally eccentric Caltech astrophysicist. He used it to make scientific breakthroughs and invent engineering devices. He said anyone who used his method would become a genius because it operationalized what it was that geniuses like himself did. He's certainly half right or more — I have seen many managers use it to come up with creative and practical ideas. These ideas often surprise us with their cleverness.

Deliberate Dreaming

Some people find that dreaming can bring ideas for solutions to problems.

James Watt, inventor of the steam engine, got a money-making idea for manufacturing lead shot during a dream. In the dream he saw rain falling and turning into hail. When he woke up he immediately set about constructing a tower with a mesh at the top of it through which molten lead would fall in drops, cooling before they hit the ground into perfectly circular balls of hardened lead.

Others have learned to deliberately dream about problems they want to solve by willing themselves to do so before they fall asleep. It's actually not hard to do this. Every now and then they find that a dream produces a solution they couldn't find while wide awake. Some psychologists claim that we are smarter when we're asleep than when we're awake. They may be right!

CREATIVE THINKING AT SONY

We conclude with a quotation from one of industry's most creative minds:

> "The human infant is born curious, but their natural curiosity gradually drains away as they grow older. I consider it my job to nurture the creativity of the people I work with because at Sony we know that a terrific idea is more likely to happen in an open, free, and trusting atmosphere than where everything is calculated, every action analyzed, and every responsibility assigned by an organization chart."
>
> Akio Morita, Sony

12

SUMMARY

Total Quality Management has been adopted in every advanced country in the world and in a number of developing economies as well. We have put it to work in governments, hospitals, schools, and universities, as well as in the private sector. TQM is, without doubt, the single most comprehensive and powerful paradigm ever to have hit the world of organizations and management.

It is a structure with many parts that assemble together into a whole that provides a different and distinct way of managing any human undertaking. It is derived from a set of powerful ideas, all of which dovetail into an extremely logical and self-consistent system.

TQM companies bear scarcely any resemblance at all to the old style of companies that they replace. They are driven by different values and ethical standards; they function in different ways; and they are predicated on different beliefs about what makes the world of work go around. Only organizations that understand the values and ideas that give life and power to TQM are in a position to make it work successfully.

NOTES

1. Stratford Sherman, "Are You as Good as the Best in the World?" *Fortune* (December 13, 1993): 95.

2. Marina Strauss, "Canada Rated Sixth in Quality of Its Manufactured Goods," *Globe and Mail*, Toronto (10 February 1994): sec. B, p. 6.

3. See Leonard L. Berry, A. Parasuraman, and Valarie Zeithaml, "Guidelines for Measuring Service Industry Quality," in *Handbook for Productivity Measurement and Improvement*, William Christopher and Carl Thor, Eds. (Portland, Ore.: Productivity Press, 1993): 4–3.1.

4. Otis Port and Geoffrey Smith, "Beg, Borrow, and Benchmark," *Business Week*, no. 3295 (November 30, 1992): 75.

5. Jim Clemmer, "The View from the Front Line," *Globe and Mail* (15 February 1994): sec. B, p. 31.

6. To learn more about Activity Based Accounting (ABC), see H. Thomas Johnson and Robert F. Kaplan, *Relevance Lost: The Rise and Fall of Management Accounting* (Cambridge, Mass.: Harvard Business School Press, 1986).

7. See Rahul Jacob, "TQM — More than a Dying Fad?" *Fortune* (October 18, 1993): 66.

8. See Leonard Sayles, *The Working Leader* (New York: The Free Press, 1993).

9. For an authoritative account, see Yoji Akao, *Hoshin Kanri: Policy Deployment for Successful TQM* (Portland, Ore.: Productivity Press, 1991).

10. See Jane Mouton and Robert Blake, *Synergogy* (San Francisco: Jossey-Bass Publishers, 1984).

11. F.D. Barrett, "Driving Quality and Productivity Improvement Ahead Through Idea Generation," in William Christopher and Carl Thor, op. cit.

FURTHER READING

This is a basic book. Since it explains the fundamental ideas only in the briefest way possible, you may want to dip into other sources later on, for example, *Handbook for Productivity Measurement and Improvement*, edited by William F. Christopher and Carl G. Thor. The handbook was published in 1993 by Productivity Press (541 NE 20th Avenue, Suite 108, Portland, Oregon 97232). It includes many articles on quality as well as productivity. In all it has 101 articles by 70 different authors. In this one book you can find almost everything you want.

For information on some of the specific tools used in implementing TQM, you may want to look into *The Memory Jogger — A Pocket Guide of Tools for Continuous Improvement* which is published by GOAL/QPC at 13 Branch Street, Methuen, Massachusetts 01844.

For a more extended exploration of TQM principles and practices, see my book *Fast Focus on TQM — A Concise Guide to Companywide Learning* (Portland, Oregon: Productivity Press, 1994).

ABOUT THE AUTHOR

Dr. F.D. (Derm) Barrett has held positions with Alcan and Canadian National Railways, and administrative and academic positions at M.I.T., York University, Queen's University, and Banff School of Advanced Management. He consults in corporate strategy, change management, management by objectives, innovation and creativity, and organization development. Dr. Barrett's clients include corporations and public institutions in North America, South America, and Europe. He holds a Ph.D. in Industrial Economics from M.I.T.

Dr. F.D. Barrett, President, Management Concepts, Limited, 31 Pine Ridge Drive, Scarborough, Ontario, Canada M1M 2X6.

The Management Master Series

The *Management Master Series* offers business managers leading-edge information on the best contemporary management practices. Written by highly respected authorities, each short "briefcase book" addresses a specific topic in a concise, to-the-point presentation, using both text and illustrations. These are ideal books for busy managers who want to get the whole message quickly.

Set 1 — Great Management Ideas

1. *Management Alert: Don't Reform—Transform!*
   Michael J. Kami

   Transform your corporation: adapt faster, be more productive, perform better.

2. *Vision, Mission, Total Quality: Leadership Tools for Turbulent Times*
   William F. Christopher

   Build your vision and mission to achieve world class goals.

3. *The Power of Strategic Partnering*
   Eberhard E. Scheuing

   Take advantage of the strengths in your customer-supplier chain.

4. *New Performance Measures*
   Brian H. Maskell

   Measure service, quality, and flexibility with methods that address your customers' needs.

5. *Motivating Superior Performance*
   Saul W. Gellerman

   Use these key factors—nonmonetary as well as monetary—to improve employee performance.

6. *Doing and Rewarding: Inside a High-Performance Organization*
   Carl G. Thor

   Design systems to reward superior performance and encourage productivity.

PRODUCTIVITY PRESS, Dept. BK, PO Box 13390, Portland, OR 97213-0390
Phone (503) 235-0600   Fax (503) 235-0909

Set 2 — Total Quality

7. *The 16-Point Strategy for Productivity and Total Quality*
   William F. Christopher and Carl G. Thor

   Essential points you need to know to improve the performance of your organization.

8. *The TQM Paradigm: Key Ideas That Make It Work*
   Derm Barrett

   Get a firm grasp of the world-changing ideas behind the Total Quality movement.

9. *Process Management: A Systems Approach to Total Quality*
   Eugene H. Melan

   Learn how a business process orientation will clarify and streamline your organization's capabilities.

10. *Practical Benchmarking for Mutual Improvement*
    Carl G. Thor

    Discover a down-to-earth approach to benchmarking and building useful partnerships for quality.

11. *Mistake-Proofing: Designing Errors Out*
    Richard B. Chase and Douglas M. Stewart

    Learn how to eliminate errors and defects at the source with inexpensive poka-yoke devices and staff creativity.

12. *Communicating, Training, and Developing for Quality Performance*
    Saul W. Gellerman

    Gain quick expertise in communication and employee development basics.

These books are sold in sets. Each set is $85.00 plus $5.00 shipping and handling. Future sets will cover such topics as Customer Service, Leadership, and Innovation. For complete details, call 800-394-6868 or fax 800-394-6286.

PRODUCTIVITY PRESS, Dept. BK, PO Box 13390, Portland, OR 97213-0390
Phone (503) 235-0600   Fax (503) 235-0909

BOOKS FROM PRODUCTIVITY PRESS

Productivity Press provides individuals and companies with materials they need to achieve excellence in quality, productivity, and the creative involvement of all employees. Through sets of learning tools and techniques, Productivity supports continuous improvement as a vision, and as a strategy. Many of our leading-edge products are direct source materials translated into English for the first time from industrial leaders around the world. Call toll-free 1-800-394-6868 for our free catalog.

Fast Focus on TQM
A Concise Guide to Companywide Learning
Derm Barrett
Finally, here's one source for all your TQM questions. Compiled in this concise, easy-to read handbook are definitions and detailed explanations of over 160 key terms used in TQM. Organized in a simple alphabetical glossary form, the book can be used either as a primer for anyone being introduced to TQM or as a complete reference guide. It helps to align teams, departments, or entire organizations in a common understanding and use of TQM terminology. For anyone entering or currently involved in TQM, this is one resource you must have.
ISBN 1-56327-049-8 / 186 pages / $20.00 / Order FAST-B243

A New American TQM
Four Practical Revolutions in Management
Shoji Shiba, Alan Graham, and David Walden
For TQM to succeed in America, you need to create an American-style "learning organization" with the full commitment and understanding of senior managers and executives. Written expressly for this audience, *A New American TQM* offers a comprehensive and detailed explanation of TQM and how to implement it, based on courses taught at MIT's Sloan School of Management and the Center for Quality Management, a consortium of American companies. Full of case studies and amply illustrated, the book examines major quality tools and how they are being used by the most progressive American companies today.
ISBN 1-56327-032-3 / 606 pages / $50.00 / Order NATQM-B243

PRODUCTIVITY PRESS, Dept. BK, PO Box 13390, Portland, OR 97213-0390
Phone (503) 235-0600   Fax (503) 235-0909

The Unshackled Organization
Facing the Challenge of Unpredictability Through
Spontaneous Reorganization
Jeffrey Goldstein
Managers should not necessarily try to solve all the internal problems within their organizations; intervention may help in the short term, but in the long run may inhibit true problem-solving change from taking place. And change is the real goal. Through change comes real hope for improvement. Goldstein explores how change happens within an organization using some of the most leading-edge scientific and social theories about change and reveals that only through "self organization" can natural, lasting change occur. This book is a pragmatic guide for managers, executives, consultants, and other change agents.
ISBN 1-56327-048-X / 208 pages / $25.00 / Order UO-B243

Achieving Total Quality Management
A Program for Action
Michel Perigord
This is an outstanding book on total quality management (TQM) — a compact guide to the concepts, methods, and techniques involved in achieving total quality. it shows you how to make TQM a companywide strategy, not just in technical areas, but in marketing and administration as well. Major methods and tools for total quality are spelled out and implementation strategies are reviewed.
ISBN 1-915299-60-7 / 392 pages / $50.00 / Order ACHTQM-B243

TO ORDER: Write, phone, or fax Productivity Press, Dept. BK, P.O. Box 13390, Portland, OR 97213-0390, phone 1-800-394-6868, fax 1-800-394-6286. Send check or charge to your credit card (American Express, Visa, MasterCard accepted).

U.S. ORDERS: Add $5 shipping for first book, $2 each additional for UPS surface delivery. We offer attractive quantity discounts for bulk purchases of individual titles; call for more information.

INTERNATIONAL ORDERS: Write, phone, or fax for quote and indicate shipping method desired. For international callers, telephone number is 503-235-0600 and fax number is 503-235-0909. Prepayment in U.S. dollars must accompany your order (checks must be drawn on U.S. banks). When quote is returned with payment, your order will be shipped promptly by the method requested.

NOTE: Prices are in U.S. dollars and are subject to change without notice.

PRODUCTIVITY PRESS, Dept. BK, PO Box 13390, Portland, OR 97213-0390
Phone (503) 235-0600   Fax (503) 235-0909

NOTES